JAY N. SMITH

The
PRAISES
of
CHRISTMAS

CHRISTMAS THROUGH THE EYES

OF THOSE WHO WERE THERE

The Praises of Christmas
Copyright © 2020 by Jay N. Smith

ISBN: 978-1-7359418-0-6 (softcover)

         978-1-7359418-1-3 (e-book)

Scripture quotations taken from the New American Standard Bible® (NASB), Copyright © 1960, 1962, 1963, 1968, 1971, 1972, 1973, 1975, 1977, 1995 by The Lockman Foundation

Used by permission. www.Lockman.org

Italics in Scripture quotations indicate emphasis added by the author.

Interior design by InkSmith Editorial Services

Cover design by David Fassett

Contents

Introduction

What memories do you have of Christmas? Perhaps they are good ones like mine—going to my grandparents' house on Christmas Eve, walking down a long staircase hand in hand with my sister on Christmas morning, and anticipating what Santa had delivered in front of the fireplace overnight.

How different, though, are the memories of those who were present during that first Christmas season: Mary, sure of God's goodness but unsure about all the implications of this baby; Zacharias, humbled by his doubts but rejoicing in God's work; the angels, marveling that their Creator would come to earth in such a vulnerable way; the shepherds, despised in society yet being first to receive the good news for all people; and finally, the elderly Simeon and Anna, rejoicing to see the young Messiah after waiting so long.

Their memories are not of candles and presents and meals and family togetherness but of God at work in a way that almost made them speechless. Thankfully, both their memories and their praises to God are preserved for us in the Bible. They all exalted God because they saw him at work in those events, each from their own perspective.

This book is my attempt to help you see the wonder and marvel of that very first Christmas. Come with me on a journey through part of the Gospel of Luke; we'll think freshly about what Christmas means through the eyes of those who were there.

Part One

Mary

Chapter One

Mary's Magnificent Praise

Mary is a model of faith rather than the object of it. In addition, she displays an extensive knowledge of God's plan of redemption through the Scriptures. She is an example of how to pray and praise God biblically.

YOU MAY HAVE HEARD THE SONG, "Mary, Did You Know?" during the Christmas season. It is a popular choice for people wanting to convey some of the mystery of Christmas, but as I have contemplated Mary's song of praise in Luke 1:46–55, my thought is not about what Mary might not have known but rather what she knew! There is evidence of what Mary knew because she was a great student of the Scriptures. She displays remarkable faith and knowledge of God's plan of redemption recorded in the Bible and is a wonderful example of how to pray and praise biblically. Wouldn't it be great if our spontaneous praise and prayers reflected as much Scripture as Mary's exaltation in this passage?

It is appropriate that we get the setting right and think through what has happened up to this point. In Luke's Gospel, prior to this moment an angel had visited Mary and explained that she would bear a son, and Mary questioned how that was to happen since she was not married yet. The angel explained that the Holy Spirit would come upon her and she would conceive. This would be a fulfillment of the promise from the prophet Isaiah that "a virgin will be with child and bear a son" (Isaiah 7:14). Mary humbly replies, "May it be done to me according to your word" (Luke 1:38). She submitted fully to God's will.

Shortly after that, she visits her cousin Elizabeth. This is a journey of about seventy miles, not a trivial trip. It took some time to get there, and she stayed for several months. You may recall that when she arrived, she greeted Elizabeth, and as Luke 1:41 says, "When Elizabeth heard Mary's greeting, the baby leaped in her womb; and Elizabeth was filled with the Holy Spirit."

Two pregnant ladies are involved in the story. In some sense both pregnancies are supernatural; they are both miracle babies. Elizabeth became pregnant by natural means, even though she was quite old, and her baby was John the Baptist, the forerunner of the promised redeemer, known as the Messiah. Even in the womb he leaps for joy knowing that the one whom he was to proclaim was near. Luke records that Elizabeth was filled with the Holy Spirit and cried out,

> Blessed are you among women, and blessed is the fruit of your womb! And how has it happened to me, that the mother of my Lord would come to me? For behold, when the sound of your greeting reached my ears, the baby leaped in my womb for joy. And blessed is she who believed that there would be a fulfillment of what had been spoken to her by the Lord." (vv. 42–45)

Elizabeth understood that Mary's response was one of faith and not of doubt.

The speech Mary made that follows in Luke 1:46–55 is often known as the *Magnificat*. It is the word that appears first in the Latin translation of the passage and refers to exalting the Lord.

As we begin to look at Mary's Magnificat, it is helpful to consider who inspired her and what influenced her thinking. It is obvious she had extensive knowledge of the Scriptures (what we now call the Old Testament) including the account of another woman of faith named Hannah. We'll consider her influence first, then we'll examine Mary's obvious knowledge of the Scriptures as a background to her Magnificat itself.

Although it seems inappropriate to dissect this beautiful expression of praise, the chapters that follow will examine each of three sections. In verses 46–49 Mary gives a personal testimony of what God has done for her. Then in verses 50–53 she recounts God's ways, both in history and in prophecy. She's looking back as well as looking forward to what God will be doing. Finally, in verses 54 and 55 Mary remembers God's covenant promises to Israel—to Abraham and his descendants forever.

Chapter Two

An Echo of Hannah's Prayer

DURING HER SEVENTY-MILE JOURNEY to visit Elizabeth, Mary may have been meditating on another significant mother in Israel: Hannah. In 1 Samuel 2, we find Hannah's prayer of praise and thanksgiving for the son that God gave her after it seemed impossible. Hannah's husband, Elkanah, loved her, but she was unable to have children. She prayed, asking the Lord for a son, and God gave her one, Samuel. He was the last of the judges of Israel and the first of the prophets as well as the one who anointed the first kings of Israel.

Looking at 1 Samuel 2:1–3, we see the first part of Hannah's prayer:

> My heart exults in the Lord;
> My horn is exalted in the Lord,
> My mouth speaks boldly against my enemies,
> Because I rejoice in Your salvation.
> There is no one holy like the Lord,
> Indeed, there is no one besides You,
> Nor is there any rock like our God.

> Boast no more so very proudly,
> Do not let arrogance come out of your mouth;
> For the Lord is a God of knowledge,
> And with Him actions are weighed.

One thing we see in Hannah's prayer that is reflected in Mary's as well is an emphasis on God's support of those who are humble and God's resistance to the proud. Indeed, we know God is opposed to the proud but gives grace to the humble (James 4:6).

Hannah's thanksgiving continues in 1 Samuel 2:4:

> The bows of the mighty are shattered,
> But the feeble gird on strength.

This is a reversal of those who are in power and out of power; the weak and feeble become the strong. God is upending circumstances.

Continuing in verse 5, she says,

> Those who were full hire themselves out for bread,
> But those who were hungry cease to hunger.
> Even the barren gives birth to seven,
> But she who has many children languishes.
> The Lord kills and makes alive;
> He brings down to Sheol and raises up.
> The Lord makes poor and rich;
> He brings low, He also exalts.
>
> He raises the poor from the dust,
> He lifts the needy from the ash heap
> To make them sit with nobles,
> And inherit a seat of honor. (vv. 5–8)

That is what has happened to us believers through the gospel. We are those who have no claim on God's promises and God's providence, but he has lifted us up and given us an inheritance in heaven forever.

Hannah finishes her prayer, saying,

> For the pillars of the earth are the Lord's,
> And He set the world on them.
> He keeps the feet of His godly ones,
> But the wicked ones are silenced in darkness;
> For not by might shall a man prevail.
> Those who contend with the Lord will be shattered;
> Against them He will thunder in the heavens,
> The Lord will judge the ends of the earth;
> And He will give strength to His king,
> And will exalt the horn of His anointed. (vv. 8–10)

We could ask, "Hannah, did you know that what you were praying was ultimately fulfilled in the Lord Jesus Christ?" and of course her answer would be no. She couldn't have fully known and realized, but it's interesting that she speaks of the Lord's anointed and of his king even before there was a king in Israel, recognizing God's kingship and foreshadowing the coming of Jesus. The same themes appear in Mary's prayer of praise.

Besides Hannah's prayer in 1 Samuel 2, it is obvious that *the whole of Scripture* influenced Mary's thinking, and that is one of the most distinguishing characteristics of Mary's Magnificat. Depending on how you count them, there are at least twelve, and maybe as many as fifteen, different Scriptures that she either quotes or alludes to through her song of praise, and most of those are from the book of Psalms. Let's look at those next.

Chapter Three

Saturated with the Scriptures

To UNDERSTAND HOW THOROUGHLY Mary's prayer of praise is filled with allusions to the Old Testament, compare the Magnificat (Luke 1:46–55) on the left to a sampling of verses that she seems to be alluding to or quoting on the right. This is not coincidental but is the product of a mind saturated with the Scriptures!

⁴⁶ And Mary said:
    "My soul exalts the Lord,
 	
⁴⁷ And my spirit has rejoiced
    in God my Savior.
	I will bless the Lord at all times;
	    His praise shall continually be in my
	    mouth.
	    My soul will make its boast in the Lord;
	    The humble will hear it and rejoice.
	    O magnify the Lord with me,
	    And let us exalt His name together.
	    (Psalm 34:1–3)
	
	And my soul shall rejoice in the Lord;
	    It shall exult in His salvation. (Psalm
	    35:9)

⁴⁸ "For He has had regard for the humble state of His bondslave; For behold, from this time on all generations will count me blessed.	For though the Lord is exalted, Yet He regards the lowly, But the haughty He knows from afar. (Psalm 138:6)
⁴⁹ "For the Mighty One has done great things for me; And holy is His name.	The Lord has done great things for us; We are glad. (Psalm 126:3) He has sent redemption to His people; He has ordained His covenant forever; Holy and awesome is His name. (Psalm 111:9)
⁵⁰ "And His mercy is upon generation after generation Toward those who fear Him.	The lovingkindness of the Lord is from everlasting to everlasting on those who fear Him, And His righteousness to children's children. (Psalm 103:17)
⁵¹ "He has done mighty deeds with His arm; He has scattered those who were proud in the thoughts of their heart.	For He has done wonderful things, His right hand and His holy arm have gained the victory for Him. (Psalm 98:1) The right hand of the Lord is exalted; The right hand of the Lord does valiantly. (Psalm 118:16) Behold, the Lord God will come with might, With His arm ruling for Him. (Isaiah 40:10)
⁵² "He has brought down rulers from their thrones, And has exalted those who were humble. ⁵³ "He has filled the hungry with good things; And sent away the rich empty-handed.	The Lord nullifies the counsel of the nations; He frustrates the plans of the peoples. (Psalm 33:10)

⁵⁴ "He has given help to Israel His servant, In remembrance of His mercy,	"But you, Israel, My servant, Jacob whom I have chosen, Descendant of Abraham My friend, You whom I have taken from the ends of the earth, And called from its remotest parts And said to you, 'You are My servant, I have chosen you and not rejected you.'" (Isaiah 41:8–9) He has remembered His lovingkindness and His faithfulness to the house of Israel. (Psalm 98:3)
⁵⁵ As He spoke to our fathers, To Abraham and his descendants forever."	I will establish My covenant between Me and you and your descendants after you throughout their generations for an everlasting covenant, to be God to you and to your descendants after you. (Genesis 17:7)

It is quite a litany of the Scriptures, and Mary knew her Bible—what we call the Old Testament—quite well. We should also worship the way Mary does, with the Scriptures and not merely with our own thoughts.

With that background, we can now consider the first section of the Magnificat, Mary's personal testimony, recorded in Luke 1:46–49.

Chapter Four

Mary's Personal Testimony

M ARY BEGINS WITH A NOTE OF PRAISE to God in Luke 1:46–47:

> And Mary said:
> "My soul exalts the Lord,
> And my spirit has rejoiced in God my Savior."

This is fitting, and I'm sure all of us would agree, "Of course we should exalt the Lord and not ourselves." But it is an apt reminder of how prone we are to exalt ourselves rather than the Lord. It is part of our fallen condition to want to promote ourselves, desiring to draw attention to what *we* have done. Yet Mary reminds us that it is appropriate to instead praise and draw attention to God.

It is clear from Mary's own testimony that she knew she herself needed a savior. She did not save herself, nor was she expecting another human to save her, but she stated, "My spirit has rejoiced in *God my Savior.*"

The theme of God as Savior is also found in Isaiah 45:21. In that passage, Isaiah is writing the Lord's words, saying,

> Declare and set forth your case;
> Indeed, let them consult together.
> Who has announced this from of old?
> Who has long since declared it?
> Is it not I, the LORD?
> And there is no other God besides Me,
> A righteous God and a Savior;
> There is none except Me.

The Lord declares that he is both *righteous* and a *savior*, and these two concepts encapsulate a mystery of theology about which volumes have been written. How can God be *both* righteous and forgive sin? You may have heard the expression that "God's justice and God's mercy met at the cross." God could only remain righteous by judging sin. He could only be merciful to sinners by providing forgiveness. He accomplished both by pouring out his wrath on our Lord Jesus Christ, who "bore our sins in His body on the cross" (1 Peter 2:24). He took the punishment our sins deserved—that is the good news of the gospel. As a result of his sacrifice, we are forgiven. God is both a righteous God and a savior.

There is a similar thought in the book of Habakkuk, one of the minor prophets. Habakkuk has a series of dialogues with the Lord; he is considering the sin of his nation and wondering why God hasn't judged it yet. God reveals to Habakkuk that judgment is coming. In fact, it is coming from the foreign nation Babylonia, which surprises Habakkuk. He wonders how God can judge his nation, Judah, by another country even more evil than his own. God explains that he will judge the Babylonians too, but first they will be his instrument against the wickedness of Judah. In Habakkuk 3:18, Habakkuk has come to accept God's judgment, and he prays,

Yet I will exult in the LORD,
I will rejoice in the God of my salvation.

Habakkuk recognized that his salvation came from God. God himself is also our savior. This is reflected in many places in the New Testament as well, particularly in Titus 3:4–5:

> But when the kindness of *God our Savior* and His love for mankind appeared, He saved us, not on the basis of deeds which we have done in righteousness, but according to His mercy, by the washing of regeneration and renewing by the Holy Spirit.

God is our savior, but he is also a judge. He acts as judge toward those who have not placed their faith in the Lord Jesus Christ, and he acts as savior to those who have trusted his work and not their own righteousness. It certainly appears that Mary is in the latter category because she said that her spirit rejoiced in God her Savior.

Mary also reflects on God's mercy in Luke 1:48, saying,

> For He has had regard for the humble state of His bondslave.

She was not extolling her own credentials or credibility or any other reason for God's choice of her. She was an ordinary young girl from an ordinary town, but God was pleased to use her for his purposes. Mary may have been without any public recognition; no one may have even noticed her, other than Joseph. It was not an unusual thing for God to choose someone like Mary, however. It is God's way.

In 1 Corinthians 1:26–29, the apostle Paul notes that this is always true in God's economy:

> For consider your calling, brethren, that there were not many wise according to the flesh, not many mighty, not many noble; but God has chosen the foolish things of the

world to shame the wise, and God has chosen the weak
things of the world to shame the things which are strong,
and the base things of the world and the despised God
has chosen, the things that are not, so that He may nullify
the things that are, so that no man may boast before God.

It is to God's glory that he chooses the ordinary, the weak,
and the inconsequential to achieve his purposes. Mary recognized that, saying in verse 48,

He has had regard for the humble state of His bondslave;
For behold, from this time on all generations will count
me blessed.

Mary is not saying all future generations should come to her
for blessing but rather all generations will look upon her and say
that she has been blessed by God. Mary is a *model* of faith rather
than the *object* of it. "All generations will count me blessed," she
says, not because of who she is but because of what God has
done. Verse 49 says,

For the Mighty One has done great things for me;
And holy is His name.

Mary is not intrinsically holy. She is being used by God to
carry out his purposes, and she willingly gives herself to his will.

Chapter Five

God's Ways in History and Prophecy

IN THE SECOND SECTION OF MARY'S Magnificat, Luke chapter 1 verses 50–53, Mary recounts God's ways in history and looks forward to what God will accomplish through the Savior that will be born. Verse 50 says,

> And His mercy is upon generation after generation
> Toward those who fear Him.

Notice that his mercy is toward those who *fear* him. We often water down this concept, but it is appropriate that we fear God in a right way. Our fear of God shows up in our reverence for him and our obedience to him.

The fear of God, rightly understood, is at the core of the gospel message. According to Revelation 14, starting in verse 6, the apostle John says,

> And I saw another angel flying in midheaven, having an eternal gospel to preach to those who live on the earth, and to every nation and tribe and tongue and people.

What is this "eternal gospel"? It must be important. Verse 7 gives the content of the angel's message:

> And he said with a loud voice, "Fear God, and give Him glory, because the hour of His judgment has come; worship Him who made the heaven and the earth and sea and springs of waters."

It is right to fear God, to honor him as the One who created all things and as the judge who will ultimately determine everyone's fate. We are pleased to have been reconciled to the Father through the Son. We are not waiting for a court appointment, a dreaded time before the judgment seat where we may argue our case before God to show how our good deeds may have outweighed our bad. Rather, we are cast entirely upon the righteousness of our Lord Jesus Christ and his payment for us. He took the punishment that our sins deserved.

Continuing in Luke 1:51, Mary says,

> He has done mighty deeds with His arm;
> He has scattered those who were proud in the thoughts
> of their heart.

May we not be proud in the thoughts of our heart! God is opposed to the proud but gives grace to the humble (James 4:6; 1 Peter 5:5). We are to humble ourselves under the mighty hand of God. He will scatter those who are proud in the thoughts of their heart. Verse 52 says,

> He has brought down rulers from their thrones,
> And has exalted those who were humble.

That thought is also reflected in Jesus's Sermon on the Mount where he says, "Blessed are the gentle [sometimes translated *meek* or *humble*], for they shall inherit the earth" (Matthew 5:5). That is part of his exaltation of those who are humble. We are humble when we recognize our proper place before God, under his control and ownership and judgment. Everything fits into place when we know who God is and we see ourselves rightly in relation to him.

Mary continues in verse 53,

> He has filled the hungry with good things;
> And sent away the rich empty-handed.

This reflects the same reversal of fortune we first saw in Hannah's prayer in 1 Samuel 2 and in many of the verses that Mary quoted. She is extolling the way that God carries out justice. There is no thought of disrupting society or establishing a human standard of justice. Mary is pointing out that God himself will do this. He is the one who scatters those who are proud, who brings down rulers, who exalts those who are humble, and who fills the hungry and sends away the rich. It is God who accomplishes those things in his timing and for his purposes. Mary extols God's ways in history and prophecy.

Chapter Six

God's Covenant Promises

IN THE THIRD SECTION OF MARY'S magnificent praise, Luke 1:54–55, Mary remembers God's covenant promises:

> He has given help to Israel His servant,
> In remembrance of His mercy,
> As He spoke to our fathers,
> To Abraham and his descendants forever.

Some people see the goodness of the gospel and the widespread opening of redemption to the gentiles (i.e., non-Jews) as evidence that God has forgotten the Jews altogether. Romans 15:8 speaks to that issue. There Paul says, "For I say that Christ has become a servant to the circumcision [that is, to the Jews] on behalf of the truth of God to confirm the promises given to the fathers."

That is what Mary is saying here. He has given help to Israel, his servant (the "circumcision" in Paul's language in Romans 15), because he remembered his mercy. God has made promises that he intends to fulfill. Then Romans 15:9 continues, "And for the Gentiles to glorify God for His mercy."

It is a marvelous both-and situation; God is able to confirm and fulfill all his promises to Israel, and he is able to open the door of redemption wide enough for those of us who are gentiles to be included as well.

God gave promises to Abraham: the land; the seed—that is, the coming one, the Messiah; and the blessing that extends to all the earth. As we will see in Luke 2, the angels proclaim that God has provided a savior, and this is good news for *all* people. He has come and redeemed us. Mary displays remarkable faith, a knowledge of God's plan of redemption throughout the Scriptures, and she is an example of how to pray and praise biblically. May his Word fill us also, that we may pray and praise according to the Scriptures.

Prayer of Reflection

Father, thank you for this word. Thank you for your servant Mary. We thank you for her obedience. We are struck by her knowledge of your Word, the Bible. Cause us to hunger for it, to be changed by it, that we may sing of you and bless you rightly. May we declare your righteous deeds, both by our lives and by recounting the deeds we see recorded in the Scriptures and the promises that we look forward to you fulfilling. We thank you for your covenants and especially for your new covenant, that our sins may be forgiven, that we may know you, that you would also write your laws on our hearts and our minds, changing us from the inside out to be your servants. We ask this in Jesus's name, amen.

Part Two

Zacharias

Chapter Seven

Zacharias's Prophetic Praise

Zacharias shows us how to praise God for his covenant faithfulness. He could see God's promises in the Abrahamic and Davidic covenants coming true, and he was excited to be part of it—and we should be too!

I F YOU'RE LIKE ME, YOU'RE SURPRISED when someone actually does what they said they would do. We are sometimes taken aback when people do what they have promised, because people often let us down. They may make a promise with the best of intentions, but later, circumstances change, and they can't fulfill their word. One thing we know with absolute certainty is that God will always fulfill his word. All his promises will come to pass, and in fact, the Scripture says that in Christ Jesus, all his promises are "yes" (2 Corinthians 1:20). Our Lord Jesus Christ is the culmination and fulfillment of all that God has promised. In the marvelous word of praise and prophecy from Zacharias recorded in Luke 1:67–79, we see that he is glorifying the Lord for his marvelous faithfulness in fulfilling his word.

But before we can even consider what Zacharias is telling us, we must remember that it is quite remarkable that he is speaking at all. In Luke 1, Zacharias, a priest, went to the temple to fulfill his duties. While he was bringing the incense offering, an angel appeared to him, to his shock and astonishment, and announced that his wife, Elizabeth, who had never been able to have children, would bear a son. Zacharias was a little uncertain, and he probably spoke too soon, doubting how it could happen. He gets a stern rebuke in Luke 1:19:

> The angel answered and said to him, "I am Gabriel, who stands in the presence of God, and I have been sent to speak to you and to bring you this good news."

The good news is about the forerunner, John the Baptist, who would go before the Messiah. But it isn't all good news; notice in Luke 1:20 that Gabriel announces the consequence of Zacharias's unbelief:

> And behold, you shall be silent and unable to speak until the day when these things take place, because you did not believe my words, which will be fulfilled in their proper time.

All God's promises will be fulfilled in their proper time even though we may think they are running late. Exactly as the angel predicted, Elizabeth gave birth to a son. When it was time to give him a name, the extended family wondered what the boy would be called. Zacharias couldn't speak, but Elizabeth knew of Gabriel's prophecy and that his name was to be John. The relatives gathered were certainly surprised about that choice because no one in the family had that name. Then they did something foolish; they tried to override the baby's mother! They asked Zacharias, who wrote on a tablet, "His name is John." They should have listened to Elizabeth, but Zacharias was able to confirm it.

When the angel said, "You shall be silent and unable to speak," it may be that not only was Zacharias unable to speak but he may also have been unable to hear. He may literally have been in silence for a little over nine months. He had a long time to contemplate what God was doing in bringing the forerunner of the Messiah. Being a priest, he certainly was aware of the Scriptures, and he may have even more intensely searched the Scriptures during that time. It may have been the only voice he could hear.

When Zacharias confirmed that his son's name was John, we are told in Luke 1:64,

> And at once his mouth was opened and his tongue loosed, and he began to speak in praise of God.

His praise has components both of forthtelling (declaring what God has done already) and foretelling (predicting what will come in the future). He does not begin his praise to God as we might expect by thanking him for his newborn son, John. Rather, in the first section, verses 68 through 75, he speaks of the Messiah and what he will accomplish. Zacharias could see the fulfillment of God's promises in the Abrahamic and Davidic covenants because of the coming of the Messiah. Then, in verses 76 to 79 he speaks to his infant son, prophesying his role as the forerunner, the one who would prepare the way for the Messiah.

Chapter Eight

Covenant Promises to David Fulfilled

LUKE 1:67–68 BEGINS THE RECORD of what Zacharias said after his tongue was loosed. He began by declaring his praise and blessing to God the Father. This praise of Zacharias is sometimes known as *Benedictus*, which is the Latin word for "blessed."

> And his father Zacharias [the father of John the Baptist] was filled with the Holy Spirit, and prophesied, saying:
>
> "Blessed be the Lord God of Israel,
> For He has visited us and accomplished
> redemption for His people."

I love his concise statement of the gospel: God visited us and accomplished redemption. The message of the gospel is one of divine accomplishment, not human achievement. That is the exact opposite of what most people think. If you ask someone, "Why do you think you will be going to heaven?" they'll often say, "I haven't done anything really bad. I think my good deeds outweigh my bad deeds"—as though there were some cosmic scale in heaven where actions are weighed. None of us can say that we have even one truly righteous deed to claim for ourselves. We cannot achieve our way to heaven. Our salvation is entirely based on what God himself has already done, just as Zacharias said: "He has visited us and accomplished redemption for His people."

Zacharias recognizes all the ways God has blessed his people in the past and especially now with the coming of the Messiah who has not even been born yet. God has visited us. He has come in person to carry out redemption for his people.

Continuing in verse 69, Zacharias says,

> And has raised up a horn of salvation for us
> In the house of David His servant.

The picture of a "horn of salvation" sounds a little odd to us. When you hear that phrase, you may think of a Viking helmet that has horns coming out of it or some other bizarre image because it is so different from the way we think and speak. In ancient Israel, horns stood for strength, the way that a big animal (like an ox) defended itself by using its horns. Horns signifying power is a common theme in Scripture. In Psalm 18:2, David says,

> The Lord is my rock and my fortress and my deliverer,
> My God, my rock, in whom I take refuge;
> My shield and the horn of my salvation, my
> stronghold.

God is the one who has the strength to accomplish salvation. Later, in Psalm 132:17, there is another reference to a horn with a promise:

> There I will cause the horn of David to spring forth;
> I have prepared a lamp for Mine anointed.

That is a messianic promise because God gave David the promise of a son yet to come, a descendant who would be the king who reigns without end. Here in Psalm 132:17, he is called the "horn of David," which refers to the strength of David, the fulfillment of all the ways that David, as the conquering king, symbolized the Messiah.

Zacharias recognizes this is what is now happening. God is causing the horn of David to spring forth, and he has "prepared a lamp" for his anointed one. John the Baptist is the forerunner, the lamp to go before the Messiah.

Zacharias mentions the "house of David" in Luke 1:69. What does that refer to? Is that a brick house? A two-story house? We think of a physical structure, but in Scripture the idea of a house means lineage, so the "house of David" refers to David's descendants. Second Samuel 7 records some of the promises that the Lord gave to David through Nathan the prophet, starting in verse 8:

> Now therefore, thus you shall say to My servant David, "Thus says the LORD of hosts, 'I took you from the pasture, from following the sheep, to be ruler over My people Israel. I have been with you wherever you have gone and have cut off all your enemies from before you; and I will make you a great name, like the names of the great men who are on the earth. I will also appoint a place for My people Israel and will plant them, that they may live in their own place and not be disturbed again, nor will the wicked afflict them any more as formerly, even from the day that I commanded judges to be over My people Israel; and I will give you rest from all your enemies.'" (vv. 8–11)

Comparing this passage with Luke 1, some of the things that Zacharias is speaking of are promises to David, part of the Davidic covenant. We see that particularly in verse 71, where Zacharias mentions "salvation from our enemies, and from the hand of all who hate us." That sounds very much like 2 Samuel

7. Skipping down to Luke 1:74, we read,

> To grant us that we, being rescued from the hand of our enemies, Might serve Him without fear,
> In holiness and righteousness before Him all our days.

Obviously, Zacharias was a student of the Scripture just as Mary was because he quotes or alludes to it. Second Samuel 7:12–13 contain the specific promise to David of an heir:

> When your days are complete and you lie down with your fathers, I will raise up your descendant after you, who will come forth from you, and I will establish his kingdom. He shall build a house for My name, and I will establish the throne of his kingdom forever.

We know from all that has come in redemptive history since then that what Nathan was speaking looked like one promise, but it was really two. There was a near fulfillment in Solomon; he built the earthly temple. That was what David wanted to do; it was how the whole exchange with Nathan started. Solomon built a house for the Lord and was a picture of the greater son of David, the Lord Jesus Christ, the one to come, who really *is* reigning forever and ever. We see the distinction between the partial fulfillment in Solomon and the ultimate fulfillment in Jesus particularly in the next verses because this cannot be true of the Lord Jesus Christ. Verses 14 through 16 of 2 Samuel 7 say,

> I will be a father to him and he will be a son to Me; when he commits iniquity, I will correct him with the rod of men and the strokes of the sons of men [the committing of iniquity was true of Solomon but not true of the Lord Jesus Christ] but My lovingkindness shall not depart from him, as I took it away from Saul, whom I removed from before you. Your house and your kingdom shall endure before Me forever; your throne shall be established forever.

The people in Israel had been waiting for generations for the fulfillment of this promise to David. Some sons of David ruled as kings, but eventually they were carried off into exile because of their disobedience. They never recovered the Davidic throne, but by faith they kept track of who was a descendant of David. That's why the opening chapters of the Gospels of Matthew and Luke include a list of names that show the lineage of the Lord Jesus Christ tracing back to David and Abraham (and in Luke's case, all the way back to Adam). The Jews kept track of who was of the lineage of David, and it turns out that both Mary and Joseph were of the house of David. Mary was the physical means by which the Lord Jesus Christ came into the world, and Joseph was the legal means by which his son could claim to be a descendant of David. Zacharias could see that the promises were coming true in the house of David, a king not just to rule and reign but one who brings salvation.

Continuing with Zacharias in Luke 1:70–71,

> As He spoke by the mouth of His holy prophets from of old—Salvation from our enemies,
> And from the hand of all who hate us.

He is recalling the promises of the messianic kingdom. Of course, the ultimate enemy is sin because that will cast the people into judgment. The horn of salvation, the Messiah, will grant relief from that ultimate enemy. Verse 72 says,

> To show mercy toward our fathers,
> And to remember His holy covenant.

God fulfills his promises. Zacharias saw the fulfillment of God's promises of old: showing mercy toward their fathers and remembering his holy covenant. Believers in Jesus are enjoying the benefits of the new covenant (Jeremiah 31:31–34; Hebrews 8:7–12) and we can be confident that the promises of God yet to be fulfilled will certainly be fulfilled. We look forward to the completion of the commitment of our Lord Jesus that "I will come again and receive you to Myself, that where I am, there you may be also" (John 14:3). The apostle Paul instructs Christians to comfort one another with the thought that "we shall always be with the Lord" (1 Thessalonians 4:17–18). Those promises will also come to pass just as the promises of Jesus's first coming were fulfilled.

Chapter Nine

Covenant Promises to Abraham Fulfilled

ZACHARIAS ALSO REMEMBERS AN EARLIER ancestor, Abraham, as he considers God fulfilling his covenant promises. God gave Abraham several promises; the first was when God called him (before he changed his name from Abram to Abraham), recorded in Genesis 12:1–3:

Now the LORD said to Abram,

> "Go forth from your country,
> And from your relatives
> And from your father's house,
> To the land which I will show you;
> And I will make you a great nation,
> And I will bless you,
> And make your name great;
> And so you shall be a blessing;
> And I will bless those who bless you,
> And the one who curses you I will curse.
> And in you all the families of the earth will
> be blessed."

We know that the promise "you shall be a blessing" to all the world is through his descendant, our Lord Jesus Christ. We are children of Abraham by faith (Romans 4:16).

In Genesis 15:5–6, the Lord confirms his promises to Abram:

> And He took him outside and said, "Now look toward the heavens, and count the stars, if you are able to count them." And He said to him, "So shall your descendants be."
>
> Then he [Abram] believed in the LORD; and He reckoned it to him as righteousness.

This is called the imputation of righteousness, which means that Abram was counted as righteous not by his works but by faith. Abram was saved, just as we are saved, by believing God, having faith in God's work—God's accomplishment—not our achievements.

In Genesis 17:3–8, the Lord continues to confirm his covenant with Abram, and changes his name to Abraham.

> Abram fell on his face, and God talked with him, saying,
>
> "As for Me, behold, My covenant is with you,
> And you will be the father of a multitude of nations.
> No longer shall your name be called Abram,
> But your name shall be Abraham;
> For I have made you the father of a multitude of nations.
>
> I will make you exceedingly fruitful, and I will make nations of you, and kings will come forth from you. I will establish My covenant between Me and you and your descendants after you throughout their generations for an everlasting covenant, to be God to you and to your descendants after you. I will give to you and to your descendants after you, the land of your sojournings, all the land of Canaan, for an everlasting possession; and I will be their God."

Zacharias remembers all these passages as he is speaking of God's faithfulness to Abraham. He is praising God for fulfilling his word, his covenant. The next section of Zacharias's outpouring of praise begins in Luke 1:73–75:

> The oath which He swore to Abraham our father,
> To grant us that we, being rescued from the hand of our
> enemies, Might serve Him without fear,
> In holiness and righteousness before Him all our days.

The letter of Hebrews says that every person is trapped by the fear of death (Hebrews 2:14–15). We are afraid of human enemies, but our ultimate fear is the judgment of our sin after death. Our Lord Jesus frees us from the fear of death so that, as Zacharias says, we "might serve Him without fear in holiness and righteousness before Him all our days." Our holiness and our righteousness are blessings of the new covenant. It is not our achievement. We don't work our way up the ladder and get to a certain level of righteousness. God declares sinners righteous because of the work of his Son, the Lord Jesus Christ. It is a divine accomplishment, not a human achievement. He has fulfilled the promise to Abraham that he would be a worldwide blessing.

Chapter Ten

John the Baptist's Role Prophesied

BEING A GOOD FATHER AND RECOGNIZING all that God is doing, Zacharias also speaks about and, remarkably, *to* his eight-day-old son. Starting in Luke 1:76, he is no longer speaking of the Messiah and the fulfillment of the Davidic and the Abrahamic covenants; now he's speaking of John the Baptist, and he accurately prophesied the role of his son as the forerunner for the Messiah. He speaks to his son, John the Baptist, who is not able to understand what his father is saying, and in his prophetic praise Zacharias declares what is true of his son:

> And you, child, will be called the prophet of the Most High;
> For you will go on before the Lord to prepare His ways."

Even his name, John, means "God is gracious." As the forerunner, he will prepare the way for the Messiah. Notice the exclusivity of his role: "You will be called *the* prophet of the Most High." Jesus spoke of the prophetic role of John the Baptist in Luke 7:26–27:

But what did you go out to see? A prophet? Yes, I say to
you, and one who is more than a prophet. This is the one
about whom it is written,

> "Behold, I send My messenger ahead of You,
> Who will prepare Your way before You."

In that passage Jesus quoted from the book of Malachi, at
the end of our Old Testament, where God promised to send a
messenger ahead of the Messiah. Jesus continues in verse 28:

> I say to you, among those born of women there is no one
> greater than John; yet he who is least in the kingdom of
> God is greater than he.

Jesus said that John is the greatest man ever born, but it is
greater still to be born *again* and enter the kingdom of God.
John the Baptist stood in the line of the Old Testament prophets,
pointing the way to Christ and salvation revealed fully in the
New Testament. Luke 3:4–6 references the book of Isaiah that
also prophesied about John:

> The voice of one crying in the wilderness,
>
> > "Make ready the way of the Lord,
> > Make His paths straight.
> > Every ravine will be filled,
> > And every mountain and hill will be brought low;
> > The crooked will become straight,
> > And the rough roads smooth;
> > And all flesh will see the salvation of God."

This clearly speaks of John the Baptist preparing the way for
the Messiah, but not all of Isaiah's prophecy came true during
the time of John the Baptist. Some of it awaits the Lord Jesus's
second coming, when literally every person will see the salvation of God.

Zacharias had been reading Isaiah and Malachi; he knew
what was coming. He continues in Luke 1:77:

> To give to His people the knowledge of salvation
> By the forgiveness of their sins.

It is not by their good deeds. It is not by what they have done but by what God has done in forgiving sins.

Continuing in verse 78,

> Because of the tender mercy of our God,
> With which the Sunrise from on high will visit us.

Here we can see God's motive—his tender mercy. It's a gracious, gentle mercy that he has extended to us in our Lord Jesus Christ.

"Sunrise" is an interesting word; it literally means "the east." The east was where the sun rose, so this word came to be associated with the sunrise, and that's why it's translated that way in the New American Standard Bible. It is not speaking of a literal sunrise but a prophetic "Son-rise," the Lord Jesus Christ himself, so the word is capitalized.

Zacharias may be alluding to Isaiah 60:1–3. There Isaiah is also speaking of the coming of the Messiah:

> Arise, shine; for your light has come,
> And the glory of the Lord has risen upon you.
> For behold, darkness will cover the earth
> And deep darkness the peoples;
> But the Lord will rise upon you
> And His glory will appear upon you.
> Nations will come to your light,
> And kings to the brightness of your rising.

The "light" and "glory" refer to the Messiah coming and revealing God's mercy. Isaiah also spoke of the brightness of the light in contrast to the darkness in Isaiah 9:2. There, he says,

> The people who walk in darkness
> Will see a great light;

> Those who live in a dark land,
> The light will shine on them.

Zacharias alluded to Isaiah 9:2 when he concluded in Luke 1:79,

> To shine upon those who sit in darkness and the shadow of death, To guide our feet into the way of peace.

Zacharias knew that the Savior was coming. Jesus declared that he is the way (John 14:6), and he will guide our feet into the way of peace.

God is not expecting us to figure it out on our own. He has revealed himself in the person of God the Son. He has revealed himself in the written word of the Scriptures to guide us into the way of peace, which refers to reconciliation with God so that we would no longer be condemned but would enjoy his forgiveness and live with him forever. Zacharias shows us how to praise God for his covenant faithfulness, knowing that he will fulfill every promise. Those who trust in the Lord Jesus Christ, the one who accomplished salvation for his people, are already experiencing the blessings of the new covenant and will enjoy them forever with him.

Prayer of Reflection

Father, we thank you for your word. It is our assurance of your kind and good intentions toward us. We thank you for bringing salvation to us, for accomplishing it by grace. We ask that you help us to think rightly of you and your truth. We long to be with you, and we know that your purposes for us will be fulfilled. We will enjoy your presence, and we know there are pleasures at your right hand forevermore. Thank you for this great praise and prophecy of Zacharias. Use it for your glory, in Jesus's name, amen.

Part Three

Angels &
Shepherds

Chapter Eleven

The Angels' and Shepherds' Praise

Even though they were looked down upon by most people, the shepherds in the fields outside Bethlehem had an important responsibility: they looked after the lambs that would be used for sacrifice at the temple in Jerusalem. They had the honor of receiving the good news before anyone else, and they rejoiced to hear it and to see the baby Jesus.

T HE STORY OF THE SHEPHERDS AND the angels is familiar to most people; it's common for children to reenact it during a Christmas program. I want to take a fresh look at it as we consider the exclamations of praise from the angels and shepherds recorded in Luke 2 and try to understand the magnitude of what is described there.

As you may recall, the government of Rome ordered a census, and that caused people to travel around the country to fulfill its requirements. The census brought Mary and Joseph to Bethlehem, which was very inconvenient because of her pregnancy. Bethlehem had been the home of David, an ancestor of both Joseph and Mary. Because of the great number of David's descendants also traveling to Bethlehem, the inn was full, nor was there room with relatives, so Joseph and Mary had to make do with what they could find. Mary gave birth to her son and laid him in a manger.

We think of the manger as a makeshift little crib, just the way it often appears in Christmas decorations, but it was actually an animal feeding trough. Mangers were often carved out of stone because food and water would cause wood to rot. The one that Mary and Joseph set baby Jesus in may not have been an ordinary manger either. It could possibly have been a rather special one, normally reserved for the lambs that would be used for sacrifice in the temple.

The sheep destined for slaughter in sacrificial ceremonies were the ones that the shepherds in the area near Bethlehem tended. Although they were part of a religious and economic system associated with the temple in Jerusalem, nothing could have prepared them for the special announcement they received one night.

Chapter Twelve

No Ordinary Sheep

In the same region [that is, near Bethlehem] there were some shepherds staying out in the fields and keeping watch over their flock by night.

–Luke 2:8

IT'S INTERESTING TO NOTE THAT THE shepherds who were in this area tending sheep were not caring for ordinary sheep, because the sheep raised between Jerusalem and Bethlehem were almost certainly dedicated to the temple sacrifices in Jerusalem. These shepherds were raising sacrificial lambs. How fascinating that an angel would appear to them, men who were familiar with the lifecycle of these sheep: from their birth to the point when they would have their throats cut, shedding their blood in a temple sacrifice ceremony to symbolize the forgiveness of sin. The deaths of those lambs pointed forward to Jesus Christ, the ultimate sacrifice for sins. The Scripture tells us in the book of Hebrews that animal sacrifices could never take away sin. In fact, because the Israelites made the sacrifice every year, it was a reminder that they were still dealing with the problem of sin (Hebrews 10:3–4).

What is sin? Sin is disobedience to our Creator, God. We have fallen short of his requirements for our worship and obedience. There is a penalty for sin that can only be paid by a perfect sacrifice. For centuries, shepherds raised sheep that were taken to the temple and sacrificed. Although they were flawless animals without blemish, they could not provide a complete sacrifice that would remove sin. Thus, John the Baptist rightly drew attention to the Lord Jesus upon seeing him, saying, "Behold, the Lamb of God who takes away the sin of the world!" (John 1:29). Jesus is the final sacrifice that fully atoned for our sin.

The shepherds were out in the fields keeping watch over the sheep, protecting them against predators and thieves. With such an important duty as looking after the lambs used in the temple sacrifices, we might assume that these shepherds were well thought of in society, but the opposite was true. Shepherds were despised people, perhaps on the lowest rung of the social ladder of the day. They were mistrusted, and in fact, shepherds were not allowed to give testimony in a court of law because they were considered dishonest. People thought that they might say whatever someone had bribed them to say.

The shepherds did not have a good reputation, and yet an angel came and appeared to them. What hope that gives to every one of us! The good news of the gospel is that it reaches everyone. It incorporates all of us because it is based on God's mercy, not on our own works or achievement.

Chapter Thirteen

Good News of Great Joy

THE SHEPHERDS WERE IN A FIELD ensuring that the sheep were safe when, as Luke 2:9 tells us,

> An angel of the Lord suddenly stood before them, and the glory of the Lord shone around them; and they were terribly frightened.

The word translated "around" refers to a circle; it is as though they were surrounded by light from the shining radiance of this messenger from heaven, and it is no wonder that they were fearful. They were literally "frightened with a great fear," which happens every time an angel appears to a human in the Scriptures. When an angel appeared to Zacharias in the temple, he was terribly frightened, and the angel told him, "Don't be afraid." An angel appeared to Mary to announce that she would give birth to the Messiah, and the angel again said to her, "Don't be afraid." Humans always need some reassurance when an angelic being becomes visible.

We find in verse 10 that the angel said to the shepherds,

> Do not be afraid; for behold, I bring you good news of
> great joy which will be for all the people.

The angel was not pronouncing judgment but rather bringing good news—great joyful news for all people. The angel continues his announcement in verse 11:

> For today in the city of David there has been born for you
> a Savior, who is Christ the Lord.

"In the city of David"—where is that? The ancient city of Bethlehem was David's birthplace, and since he was so prominent as the honored king of Israel, the town took its name and its reputation from David. Thus, it became the city of David.

The Scriptures tell us that the Lord declared to David, "I took you from the pasture, from following the sheep, to be ruler over My people Israel" (2 Samuel 7:8). David had grown up as a shepherd near Bethlehem. Could it be that he tended sheep in the area where the shepherds were that night? Perhaps David composed Psalm 23 in the same meadow. David tended sheep, but God made him the king. Later, shepherds were in the same area, and an angel came to announce good news about another king; a Savior born in the city of David—that is, in Bethlehem.

A Savior is one who saves, delivers, or rescues someone in need. In our world with so many conveniences and things that are easy for us, you may find yourself asking, "What do I need to be saved from?" From the Bible's perspective, our primary problem is not ecological; it is not an economic disaster, nor is it warfare or disease. Ultimately, we need to be saved from the wrath of God. We need to be saved from God himself! In addition to his love and grace, God is also holy and cannot tolerate the rebellion of his creatures. We must be saved from the righteous pouring out of God's wrath upon those who have rebelled against him. We are all born in a condition of indifference and defiance toward God. We came by it naturally. We inherited it from our parents, and we have piled on top of it our own sins, our own rebellion against God. We need a savior. We need someone to rescue us, and God has done it! He saved us from himself. He provided a savior to protect us from his own righteous wrath, and the angels declared the good news: "There has been born for you a Savior, who is Christ the Lord."

The word *Christ* is a Greek word translated from the Hebrew word for "Messiah." He is the promised one, predicted by the prophets of Israel hundreds of years before. He came to do God's will, rescuing his people.

Lord means "the king," "the sovereign," "the ultimate ruler." The shepherds would have easily understood that calling him the Lord meant that he is God himself. The Messiah is the Savior, and he is the Lord, the sovereign one. The angels told the shepherds that the Savior had been born for them, and he was born for you and me as well. He was not born for his own benefit; he was born *for us.*

The book of Hebrews tells us that the Lord Jesus took on flesh so he could represent us and offer himself as the ultimate sacrifice for sins (Hebrews 2:14–15). He did that out of his love to redeem those who are estranged from God. He was born because of his love for people. He has been born for *you.* Perhaps you're not sure where you stand with God. You may be asking, "What is my relationship to God? Are my sins forgiven?" They are if you're trusting not in his birth but in what he accomplished on the cross. He came like a lamb that he might be slain—not in the temple but on the cross. Through his suffering, the Lord Jesus paid the sin debt you and I owe. We can be saved—rescued from God's wrath—if we put our trust and confidence in what he has accomplished. "Today," the angel said, "in the City of David there has been born for you a Savior." He is the Messiah, and he is the Lord.

Chapter Fourteen

A Sign of Things to Come

WHEN THE ANGEL SAID THAT THERE was good news of great joy for all people, the shepherds knew it was true, but it would have been difficult for them to understand how a baby who has just been born could be the Savior. He wouldn't be immediately saving and ruling, so in the meantime, how could they know for sure? That is what the angel explains next, in Luke 2:12:

> This will be a sign for you: you will find a baby wrapped in cloths and lying in a manger.

We find a common pattern in prophetic messages. After something marvelous is announced—something that may take a long time to accomplish—it will be paired with a sign that will occur sooner in time. If the sign comes true, everyone can have confidence that the greater, later thing will also come true.

The angel gave the shepherds a sign. When they saw the sign fulfilled, they would have certainty that the child really was the

Savior, Christ the Lord. What was the sign? "A baby wrapped in cloths and lying in a manger." Now a baby wrapped in cloths was not an unusual thing, but no one would put their baby in a feeding trough!

Beyond that, it may not have been an ordinary feeding trough. During some recent excavations in Israel, archeologists unearthed a tower in the region near Bethlehem which was used by the priests to look after the lambs being raised for sacrifice in the temple. When the priests saw that a ewe was nearing the time to give birth, they would bring it to the base of the tower, a safe area. If the ewe's lamb was flawless—one that would be perfect for the temple sacrifices—they would wrap it up in cloths. They did that to protect it so it wouldn't get any blemishes. And they would put it in the manger so it wouldn't get trampled or bruised by any of the other animals. Could the Lamb of God have been laid in *that* manger? Could the symbolism be that strong? We have no way to know for sure, but perhaps the only place available for Mary to give birth was at the base of the tower where the sacrificial lambs were born.

Jesus was wrapped as babies are—and in the same way that flawless sacrificial lambs were wrapped. And like them, he was placed in a manger. That may have been the sign the shepherds were looking for. With no further direction, they may have known exactly where to go to find a child laid in a manger. It is a fascinating thing to speculate about, but certainly we know that this child, this flawless son, was the Son of Man and the Son of God, the perfect sacrifice for sins. He had to be born so that he could die, just like those lambs that the shepherds were looking after.

The angel gave them a sign, something that would quickly prove the truth of the announcement of good news for all people: a baby wrapped in cloths and lying in a manger, not in a crib as they would normally expect. The shepherds may have just begun to recover from seeing an angel and hearing the news—and the accompanying sign—when it seemed that *all* the angels joined in praise.

Chapter Fifteen

Where Did All Those Angels Come From?

A FTER ONE ANGEL HAD EXPLAINED THE good news to the shepherds and given them assurance through a sign, Luke 2:13–14 tells us,

> And suddenly there appeared with the angel a multitude of the heavenly host praising God and saying,
>
> > "Glory to God in the highest,
> > And on earth peace among men with whom
> > He is pleased."

You may ask, "Where did they come from?" We know they came from heaven, but perhaps they were there all along and suddenly became visible. There are supernatural realities we cannot perceive with our natural senses. So, while the shepherds saw one angel at first, there may have been a multitude there all along and then suddenly their true glory shone.

The angels declared "peace among men with whom He is pleased." The only way for God to be pleased with us is for the problem of sin to be resolved. The Messiah came to remove the barrier of sin so that we can have peace with God. He did that through the work he accomplished on the cross.

The angels declared, "Glory to God in the highest," a proclamation which should be in our hearts also because that is a right response to God. We are to give glory to God alone, not to ourselves. We are not to praise other people but God only.

When the angels said, "Glory to God in the highest," they were glorifying God. We also give glory to God as we shine the spotlight of our affection and admiration on the only One worthy of our devotion. The angels praised God for what he was doing, and as suddenly as they came, they returned to heaven.

Chapter Sixteen

The Shepherds Seek the Savior

IMAGINE BEING ONE OF THE SHEPHERDS who had just heard good news of great joy and seen a chorus of angels. What would you do next? Luke 2:15 tells us,

> When the angels had gone away from them into heaven, the shepherds began saying to one another, "Let us go straight to Bethlehem then, and see this thing that has happened which the Lord has made known to us."

The angel announced the news and then gave them a sign, something to look for. The shepherds were looking for the sign because they knew if they found it, the announcement of the Messiah, a Savior who is Christ the Lord, would come true as well. Verses 16 and 17 tell us,

> So they came in a hurry and found their way to Mary and Joseph, and the baby as He lay in the manger. When they had seen this, they made known the statement which had been told them about this Child.

They saw the sign, a baby lying in a manger, a place normally used as a feeding trough. They knew what the angel told them was coming true.

Apparently, other people were present at this point. Verse 18 says,

> And all who heard it wondered at the things which were told them by the shepherds.

Those lowly shepherds, forbidden to testify in court, now testified to those who were gathered, saying that the Lord is doing great things. The angel told the shepherds about a sign, and it came to pass, so they knew the baby truly was the Savior, Christ the Lord.

Luke notes Mary's reaction in verse 19:

> But Mary treasured all these things, pondering them in her heart.

Mary had memories of a visit from the angel Gabriel. She knew what happened to Elizabeth—her providential pregnancy—and to Zacharias. Mary had just given birth to her own baby, and then the shepherds came, saying they had seen an angel. Mary remembered all these things and thought through them in her heart.

Luke concludes this section in verse 20 with the praise of the shepherds as they returned to their field; they still had sheep to tend.

> The shepherds went back, glorifying and praising God for all that they had heard and seen, just as had been told them.

The shepherds were overjoyed that the message from the angel was confirmed—the Messiah had been born! They glorified God, honoring the only One worthy of their devotion. Their experience didn't go to their heads; it didn't cause them to be proud. They praised God because it was obvious that only God could arrange the circumstances of the baby's birth and send the angels to announce it.

Did their praise include thanksgiving to God that they were the ones who received the announcement and not the religious leaders in Jerusalem? Did it strike them that they were privy to the good news of great joy before other people were? They had a humble response, and the fact that they directed their praise to God shows they understood that something massively bigger than the birth of a baby happened that night.

What about you? Is Christmas more than a big celebration about the birth of one baby? The shepherds understood that Jesus's *birth* was not the most important thing; it was his identity as Savior. You can trust the Lord Jesus Christ in his work, not as a baby but as the Lamb of God. You must believe that he accomplished redemption at his death and that his work was validated at his resurrection. Death could not hold him. He completed his sacrifice and then rose from the dead. Now he saves those who cast themselves entirely upon him, trusting in his finished sacrifice. We call this message the *gospel*, which means "good news," just as the angels said.

Those who believe echo the angel, saying to one another, "I bring you good news of great joy." They enjoy reconciliation and peace with God, and adoption into God's family forever. For those who trust in the work of his Son, his payment on the cross for sin, there truly has been born a Savior, Christ the Lord.

God himself has come to visit us—but not to tell us how to live a good life or even teach us religious principles. He did not come merely to be a good example or even to heal people. He came specifically as a lamb that he might offer himself as a sacrifice. The Scriptures refer to Jesus *giving himself* (Galatians 1:4;

2:20; Ephesians 5:2, 25; 1 Timothy 2:6). His life was not torn away from him; he offered it freely as a sacrifice for us. We do not deserve it. We have no claim on God's mercy. He offered himself as a sacrifice that we might be saved from his wrath. This is indeed good news of great joy—a Savior, who is Christ the Lord.

Prayer of Reflection

Father, we thank you for this great news. We thank you for all that you did to prepare the way for your Son, for all the prophecies coming true at the time of his birth. Lord Jesus, thank you for coming to the earth and offering yourself freely as our sacrifice. You came for us. We are in awe, and we marvel. I pray that you would call many to yourself through the truth of your birth. I pray that people would trust in what you accomplished on the cross, bearing the penalty of our sins. Thank you for being our Savior and Redeemer that we may be adopted into your family forever. In the name of our Savior and King, the Lord Jesus Christ, amen.

Part Four

Simeon & Anna

Chapter Seventeen

Simeon's and Anna's Praise

Simeon and Anna were two of a small number of faithful believers looking for the Messiah's arrival, and they were blessed to see him in fulfillment of their faith-filled expectations. Although his coming was the hope of all who trusted in God, it was also a sign of God's final judgment, which will divide humanity into two eternal destinies.

AFTER THE UNUSUAL BIRTH OF MARY's baby and the visit of the shepherds, Mary and Joseph probably experienced the normal life of first-time parents: caring for the baby, changing diapers, and obeying all the provisions in God's law for parents, including the dedication of their baby at the temple. They had no idea what further supernatural surprises were in store for them there. God reminded them through Simeon and Anna that their child was more than just another baby boy. Simeon gave them a warning that this baby would cause great controversy.

We live in a time of sharp division. The nation is struggling over polarizing opinions. Who do you think is the most divisive person right now? What about over the last decade or perhaps the last century? There are controversial figures in every age, and yet, from the perspective of a hundred or even a thousand years later, most of their lives are summarized by footnotes in history books. They don't matter much. But one person is ultimately divisive, the One over whom all humanity will be separated in opinion. That person, of course, is the Lord Jesus Christ.

It may seem unusual to consider a little baby as the source of strife and division, yet that is what we see, particularly in the prophecy of Simeon. Simeon praises God, rejoicing at the coming of the Messiah, and then predicts trouble to come. Though the coming of the Messiah was the fulfillment of prophecy about God's salvation, it was also a sign reminding people about their fate.

As we consider the text of Luke 2:25–38, we'll look at three parts. First, in verses 25–32, Simeon longed to witness the fulfillment of God's promises to Israel; the Lord was gracious to him and sustained him until he could see the Messiah with his own eyes. Then, in verses 33–35, Simeon predicted that all humanity would be divided because of this child. Finally, in verses 36–38, Anna's devotion was rewarded.

As we consider Luke's record of Simeon and Anna meeting the baby Jesus at the temple, certain questions arise: Who was Simeon, and why was he particularly looking for the Messiah? How did Anna happen to be at the temple that day?

Chapter Eighteen

A Righteous and Devout Man

WHAT WAS THE ATMOSPHERE IN Jerusalem at the time of Jesus's birth? It was remarkably like it is now. The mainstream body of religion was characterized by hypocrisy, legalism, and unbelief, just as it is now. In Jerusalem, only a few people were truly trusting in God's word and the coming of the Messiah. Only a few were looking forward to a literal fulfillment of God's word—but there were a few.

In the broad sweep of what is called Christianity in our day, there is much hypocrisy, shallowness, and legalism on one hand, and total rejection of the reliability of the Scriptures on another. But there is a remnant of true believers. We should not be proud of being part of that remnant but instead praise God that there *is* a remnant.

Simeon and Anna were in a minority among those practicing Judaism. Our text picks up in Luke 2:25:

> And there was a man in Jerusalem whose name was Simeon; and this man was righteous and devout.

You may recall that Simeon was the name of one of the twelve tribes, the sons of Jacob. He was dedicated and careful in his practice of God's law. Notice also in Luke 2:25 that Simeon was

> looking for the consolation of Israel; and the Holy Spirit was upon him.

What was the "consolation"? Why was he looking for it? *Consolation* means comfort. Simeon was looking for the comfort of his people, Israel, through the coming of the Messiah. The basis of his looking for consolation, at least in part, was Isaiah 40:1–2.

> "Comfort, O comfort My people," says your God.

> "Speak kindly to Jerusalem;
> And call out to her, that her warfare has ended,
> That her iniquity has been removed,
> That she has received of the Lord's hand
> Double for all her sins."

In Isaiah 40, God is announcing comfort and peace with Israel; we know that it is through the coming of the Messiah who will take away the punishment for sin. If you glance at the next verse in Isaiah 40, verse 3, you'll see a prediction about John the Baptist's ministry:

> A voice is calling,

> "Clear the way for the Lord in the wilderness;
> Make smooth in the desert a highway for our God."

He would clear the way, making a path for the Lord. John was the forerunner. Isaiah 40 links the verses on consolation with the coming forerunner for the Messiah. Simeon was looking for comfort from God because he knew that the sin problem had to be dealt with fully and finally, and he saw this beginning to happen.

Why was he looking for the consolation of Israel at *this* time? Luke 2:25 states that "the Holy Spirit was upon him," and perhaps the Holy Spirit helped him see another ancient prophecy coming true, this time from the book of Daniel.

Chapter Nineteen

Was Simeon Informed
by Daniel's Prophecy?

T HERE ARE FASCINATING PROPHECIES in the book of Daniel. Chapter 9 opens with Daniel saying, "I, Daniel, observed in the books [scrolls] the number of the years which was revealed as the word of the Lord to Jeremiah the prophet for the completion of the desolations of Jerusalem, namely, seventy years" (v. 2). Daniel looked in the Scripture and calculated that the time of exile prophesied by Jeremiah was almost over. Daniel took God's word seriously, and he believed that it would be fulfilled literally.

Based on his confidence in God's word, he began praying, saying, "Lord, we have sinned. You were right in sending us into exile." He prostrated himself and prayed to God on behalf of his whole nation, even for sins he himself did not commit. Then the Lord answered him in a dramatic way—the angel Gabriel came and gave him a message. That name should immediately register in our minds, because Gabriel is part of the Christmas story also. He was the angel that came to Mary as well as to Zacharias.

He may also have been the angel that appeared to the shepherds. We can't know for sure, but we do know Gabriel was involved in announcing the coming of the Messiah.

Simeon may have been thinking about the message that Gabriel gave to Daniel many years before. The message from Gabriel to Daniel is recorded in Daniel 9, starting in verse 24:

> Seventy weeks [sets of seven years] have been decreed for your people and your holy city, to finish the transgression, to make an end of sin, to make atonement for iniquity, to bring in everlasting righteousness, to seal up vision and prophecy and to anoint the most holy place.

The original Hebrew word translated "weeks" means "seven." Our words *pair* and *dozen* are similar in the sense that they stand for a group of objects and need another word to describe the objects more specifically, like *shoes* or *eggs*. The angel Gabriel is telling him that 70 sevens have been declared, because each "week" refers to a group of seven. If you're good at math, you can multiply that out and determine that it refers to 490 of something, but what? Since this is dealing with history, we understand that Gabriel is referring to 490 years.

Then it gets a little more detailed. Notice in Daniel 9:25, Gabriel continues,

> So you are to know and discern that from the issuing of a decree to restore and rebuild Jerusalem until Messiah the Prince there will be seven weeks [i.e., sevens] and sixty-two weeks [sevens]; it will be built again, with plaza and moat, even in times of distress.

Anyone could determine when Messiah the Prince would be coming based on the decree to restore and rebuild Jerusalem. In fact, scholars have crunched the numbers by looking at history and understanding the calendars people used, and it works out that the coming of Messiah the Prince after the seven sevens and sixty-two sevens was the date we call Palm Sunday, the day that Jesus rode into Jerusalem to much praise and acclaim.

We cannot predict the second coming of Christ with this kind of mathematical precision, but it appears that God intended for people to know the date of his first coming through Daniel's prophecy. Simeon, a devout man who had the Holy Spirit upon him, surely knew the prophecy from Daniel. He knew the history of his people, so he would likely have been able to calculate how many years it had been since the decree. Simeon could have read this prophecy and calculated that the time of the Messiah's appearance was near—about thirty-three years away (the length of Jesus's earthly life). I think he sensed, like Daniel so many years before, that it was almost time for the prophecy to be fulfilled. Daniel determined the end of the exile based on the prophecy of Jeremiah; Simeon may have determined the time of the Messiah's coming based on the prophecy that Daniel received from Gabriel.

Perhaps Simeon thought that since the Messiah would be their king, he would appear as a full-grown man. Based on the year specified in the prophecy from Daniel, Simeon may have thought it likely that the Messiah had already been born. Maybe the Holy Spirit even told Simeon that! Note that Luke 2:26 says,

> And it had been revealed to him by the Holy Spirit that he would not see death before he had seen the Lord's Christ.

The Holy Spirit revealed to him that he would see the Messiah in his lifetime. We have the comfort that one day we will see God after we die, but Simeon had an assurance from the Holy Spirit that he would not die before he saw the Messiah. He read the Scriptures carefully, and he took them literally. He was looking for the comfort that Isaiah had predicted, and perhaps the reason he was looking for the Messiah at *that* time was because of the message of Gabriel to Daniel.

Chapter Twenty

Simeon's Desire Fulfilled

THE FIRST PART OF LUKE 2:27 speaks of Simeon, saying,

And he came in the Spirit into the temple.

I don't think this is telling us he floated into the temple with his feet not touching the ground but rather that he was meditating on God's word; he was prayerful as he was led by God into the temple. Perhaps the Holy Spirit had nudged him, saying, "Today's the day. Go now. Walk to the temple."

In the temple complex were the spaces God had specified to Moses, including the Holy Place and the Holy of Holies, but those were surrounded by layers of other buildings and courtyards. The outermost area was a place everyone could come called the Court of the Gentiles; the Jewish religious leaders had restricted the gentiles to that courtyard and no farther inside under penalty of death. Beyond that was an inner court called the Court of the Women; the temple leaders also made up a rule that the women could go to that point but no farther. Neither of these restrictions were in the Bible; they just added them to God's law.

All the events that Luke records about Simeon and Anna most likely took place in the Court of the Women. Continuing in Luke 2:27–32, Luke writes,

> And when the parents brought in the child Jesus, to carry out for Him the custom of the Law, then he [Simeon] took Him into his arms, and blessed God, and said,
>
>> "Now Lord, You are releasing Your
>> bond-servant to depart in peace,
>> According to Your word;
>> For my eyes have seen Your salvation,
>> Which You have prepared in the presence of
>> all peoples,
>> A Light of revelation to the Gentiles,
>> And the glory of Your people Israel."

The Holy Spirit orchestrated the meeting so they could all be there at the right time. It says that Mary and Joseph were there "to carry out for Him the custom of the Law." We understand from the law that on the eighth day every male child was to be circumcised. There was also a time of ritual impurity for the mother that added another thirty-three days. The law of Moses specified a sacrifice that a woman must bring to the temple in recognition of the completion of that ceremonial uncleanness (Leviticus 12:2–8). The requirement was to bring a lamb, but if she couldn't afford a lamb, she could bring a pair of turtledoves or pigeons. Luke mentions earlier in chapter 2 that Mary and Joseph took advantage of that provision for the poor, for they could not afford a lamb.

The "custom of the Law" that Luke notes refers to a law recorded in the book of Exodus in which God claimed all the firstborn males. God said that every firstborn is his and that they were to redeem their sons (Exodus 13:11–15). In other words, the Israelites had to buy back their firstborn sons from God because he claimed rightful ownership of every firstborn son. Mary and Joseph were precisely following the requirement in the law to redeem their son and to recognize the end of Mary's ceremonial uncleanness. They were carrying out those things in the temple that day when Simeon met them. Perhaps they were looking for a priest to bless the child and he was right there. Simeon blessed God and prayed the prayer recorded in verses 29 to 32, acknowledging, "It's time for me to go. You've accomplished what you promised to me in your word." It is amazing how ready he is to die. Simeon had clung to a promise that the Holy Spirit had given to him, specifically, that he would not die before he saw the Messiah. He realizes it has happened, so now he is ready to die.

Notice in verse 30 that Simeon said,

> "My eyes have seen Your salvation."

He saw the Savior who would provide salvation. He didn't see Jesus on the cross, and quite likely Simeon didn't live that long, but he saw with eyes of faith the baby Jesus and knew that he was the Messiah. Simeon knew that Jesus was the Promised One who would bring all the purposes of God to fruition, including God's promise to Abraham that he would be a blessing to all the nations (Genesis 12:3).

Notice the worldwide scope of Simeon's understanding of the salvation he saw, recorded in verses 31 and 32:

> Which You have prepared in the presence of all peoples,
> A Light of revelation to the Gentiles,
> And the glory of Your people Israel."

God's desire has always been for a worldwide people of faith. Not just for one nation, not just Israel; it is a plan of salvation for every nation.

Isaiah 45:22 expresses a similar thought:

"Turn to Me and be saved, all the ends of the earth."

This is a call of universal scope on God's part. Later, in Isaiah 52:10, it says,

> The Lord has bared His holy arm
> In the sight of all the nations,
> That all the ends of the earth may see
> The salvation of our God.

It is as though God says, "I've got some work to do, so I'm going to roll up my sleeves." God bared his arm to accomplish salvation. The aim is that all the ends of the earth may see the salvation of our God. That is the basis of our Lord's Great Commission in Matthew 28:19–20:

> Go therefore and make disciples of all the nations, baptizing them in the name of the Father and the Son and the Holy Spirit, teaching them to observe all that I commanded you; and lo, I am with you always, even to the end of the age.

The scope is all nations, to the ends of the earth. It is a worldwide plan of salvation. Simeon recognized that, although many of his contemporaries did not. Someone had put up a wall preventing the gentiles from going past a certain point in the temple. That was an artificial barrier. The apostle Paul says God has knocked it down; he has removed the barrier because he is joining, in his new covenant people, the Jews and the gentiles (Ephesians 2:13–16). Simeon anticipated that.

Look again at the wonderful "both-and" in verse 32:

> A Light of revelation to the Gentiles,
> And the glory of Your people Israel.

This is like Romans 15:8–9, which we looked at earlier. He says there,

> For I say that Christ has become a servant to the circumcision [that is, to the Jews] on behalf of the truth of God to confirm the promises given to the fathers, and for the Gentiles to glorify God for His mercy.

Christ became a servant to confirm the promises to the Jews *and* to welcome the gentiles. God's intent is for all kinds of people—Jews and gentiles—to come to faith in Christ and trust him for their salvation.

Simeon also spoke of a "light of revelation," alluding to Isaiah 49:6:

> It is too small a thing that You [that is, the Messiah]
> should be My Servant
> To raise up the tribes of Jacob and to restore the preserved ones of Israel;
> I will also make You a light of the nations
> So that My salvation may reach to the end of the earth.

It is not a large enough scope to be the Savior of the Jews only; it must be a worldwide salvation. Isaiah's "light of the nations" is reflected in Simeon's prayer; he understands that the Messiah will be "a light of revelation to the Gentiles." This is such a high note of praise that it seems like the encounter should end there, but Simeon has more to say. After realizing that many prophecies from the past are coming true, he himself will utter a prophecy about the future.

Chapter Twenty-One

Division Prophesied

S IMEON HAD THE UNIQUE PRIVILEGE of seeing the Messiah
before he died, but in the next verses, he prophesied about
coming division. Luke 2:33 says,

> And His father and mother were amazed at the things
> which were being said about Him.

They knew God was at work, and yet coming to the temple
flooded with people and having Simeon come and bless their
child and pray for them was remarkable. Notice Luke 2:34:

> And Simeon blessed them and said to Mary His mother.

Simeon spoke directly to Mary. What about Joseph? We don't
know for sure, but it appears that sometime after the Lord Jesus was age twelve, Joseph was no longer present (most likely
because he died), and Jesus became the caretaker of his mother
and the leader of his brothers and sisters. At his death, the Lord
Jesus entrusted the care of his mother to the apostle John. From

the cross he said to Mary, "Behold, your son!" and to John, "Behold, your mother!" (John 19:26–27).

Joseph did not live to see Jesus's ministry—or his death—so Simeon gives this special message only to Mary. He says, in verse 34 of Luke 2,

> Behold, this Child is appointed for the fall and rise of many in Israel, and for a sign to be opposed—and a sword will pierce even your own soul—to the end that thoughts from many hearts may be revealed.

Simeon takes an ominous tone in his prophecy, speaking of opposition, a sword piercing Mary's soul, and the curious phrase "this Child is appointed for the fall and rise of many." He implies that Jesus will have a divisive role in the destiny of people; he will divide people!

The Old Testament prophets spoke of the Messiah as a stone, a stone of stumbling (Isaiah 8:14–15) and the stone that the builders rejected (Psalm 118:22). That rejection came to pass in Jerusalem. He was the stone that the builders rejected. The builders—the Sadducees, Pharisees, and the scribes—rejected him. Around forty years after Jesus's death and resurrection, the Romans, under the emperor Titus, destroyed the temple and ended the influence and authority of the builders who rejected the stone while the apostles preached and trained others to take the gospel to the world. Jesus spoke of himself as a stone, saying, "He who falls on this stone [i.e., on himself] will be broken to pieces; but on whomever it falls, it will scatter him like dust" (Matthew 21:44).

How we respond to that stone, the Lord Jesus Christ, determines our eternal destiny. Those who fall on the stone, casting themselves upon God for his mercy, will be saved. Those who fall on the stone will be broken in pride and self-confidence but not destroyed. Those who refuse to fall *on* the stone will be crushed *by* the stone. There are two destinies: one for those who trust in Jesus, described by Jesus as falling on the stone, and one for those who refuse to trust in him, described by Jesus as being scattered like dust.

Jesus divides all humanity into those two groups. He said, "Do you suppose that I came to grant peace on earth? I tell you, no, but rather division" (Luke 12:51). Matthew 10:34 similarly records that Jesus said, "Do not think that I came to bring peace on the earth; I did not come to bring peace, but a sword." King Jesus will judge each of us based solely on where we stand in relation to him. Is he your Savior or your Judge? That is the question.

In speaking of "the fall and rise of many in Israel," Simeon may be alluding to the resurrection because of this passage in Daniel 12:1-2:

> There will be a time of distress such as never occurred since there was a nation until that time; and at that time your people, everyone who is found written in the book, will be rescued. Many of those who sleep in the dust of the ground will awake, these to everlasting life, but the others to disgrace and everlasting contempt.

Daniel prophesied that every person would rise from the dead, but it will not be the same for everyone. Those who are "found written in the book" will be raised to everlasting life, but the others will suffer shame and everlasting scorn.

Simeon also notes that Jesus is "a sign to be opposed." A sign is something happening soon that points to the certainty of something else occurring later. The coming of the Messiah was a sign that all God's promises *and* all God's judgment would surely come to pass. That is why he is "a sign to be opposed"; many do not want the righteousness and the judgment of God. They are those who will be crushed by the stone when it falls on them.

The baby is not only "a sign to be opposed" but also a source of anguish for Mary. Simeon tells her in Luke 2:35,

> And a sword will pierce even your own soul—to the end that thoughts from many hearts may be revealed.

That will happen at God's throne of judgment; the hidden thoughts and motives of the heart will be revealed. Hebrews 4:12 tells us that the word of God does that now—it pierces into the heart to judge motives and inner thoughts.

Mary would later experience a unique pain like a sword piercing her soul. It's difficult, if not impossible, for us to imagine the anguish of a mother watching her son be publicly executed, but if the mother knew that her son was guilty it might temper the pain a bit. Mary experienced the anguish of seeing her firstborn son die, publicly executed in shame, and she knew he was completely innocent.

If there is anyone who knows the truth about us, it is our mother. She may talk us up to everybody else, but Mom knows what's really there. She has known us from childhood, seeing our sin nature come out. Mary didn't see that in Jesus because he had no sin nature. The torment of seeing her innocent son die was like a sword piercing her own soul.

Simeon had the unique privilege of seeing the Messiah before he died, and Mary had plenty of things to think about already, but more was to come. God had one more devoted servant at the temple that day who recognized who the Child was.

Chapter Twenty-Two

Anna's Devotion Rewarded

S IMEON WAS NOT THE ONLY PERSON looking for the Messiah; there were others, and one of them was a godly woman who was often at the temple. Verse 36 of Luke 2 says,

> And there was a prophetess, Anna the daughter of
> Phanuel, of the tribe of Asher.

Asher was one of the tribes of the Northern Kingdom, Israel, after it split from Judah in the south. Some people think the people of Asher lost their identity during the exile, but Anna is described as being "of the tribe of Asher," so we know some people from the Northern Kingdom preserved the records of their tribal heritage well beyond the exile. As the Northern Kingdom slid into idolatry and then exile, some of the people migrated to the Southern Kingdom, so that may explain the presence of someone from the tribe of Asher being in Jerusalem.

Continuing in Luke's account, in verses 36–37, it says of Anna,

> She was advanced in years and had lived with her husband seven years after her marriage, and then as a widow to the age of eighty-four. She never left the temple, serving night and day with fastings and prayers.

She must have eaten at some point, but she regularly fasted and prayed. In verse 38 Luke notes the impeccable timing of the Holy Spirit:

> At that very moment she came up and began giving thanks to God, and continued to speak of Him to all those who were looking for the redemption of Jerusalem.

While Simeon was giving his praise and his prophecy of division, Anna worshiped because she knew that the baby was the Messiah. This was not a private devotion, though, because Luke records that she spoke of Jesus to everyone in the faithful remnant. Anna and Simeon were part of a small group who took God's word seriously and were looking forward to the coming of the Messiah. She gossiped the gospel—she talked to everyone who was looking for the redemption of Jerusalem, looking for the Messiah to come and redeem them. She was saying, "He's here. I've seen Him in the temple." Her long-time devotion was rewarded by seeing the Messiah.

Simeon and Anna were orchestrated by God to bear testimony of the coming of the Messiah, the hope of all who truly trusted God. His coming was also a sign of God's final judgment, which will divide humanity into two eternal destinies.

Prayer of Reflection

Father, thank you for this word of prophecy and comfort and warning of what is to come. We pray that you would cause us to be more devoted to you and your cause. Stir in us love for your Word, and grant that we would take it seriously and proclaim the offer of salvation to all people. We pray that all will trust in his completed work, that all would cast themselves on the Lord Jesus. In his name we pray, amen.

Conclusion

THANK YOU FOR COMING ON THIS journey with me through the praises of Mary, Zacharias, the angels and shepherds, Simeon, and Anna as recorded in Luke's Gospel. I hope you have a new sense of awe and wonder about Christmas, about the ultimate gift that God has given, and the intricate plans laid over the centuries before to prepare the way for his Son to come to the earth—God with us!

You may be wondering, though, what it means to *you*. It is an epic story of long-ago prophecies fulfilled and joyful rejoicing, but what does it mean for you right now? Only part of the answer is found in the stories of Jesus's birth; the rest is in the reason that he came. Later in Luke 19:10, Jesus explains his purpose in coming, saying,

> For the Son of Man has come to seek and to save that which was lost.

That may be the clearest statement from the lips of Jesus about why he came to earth, why there is a Christmas to celebrate. It was a rescue mission! Apart from him, you and I are hopelessly lost. We may have the finest GPS-enabled devices, but in light of eternity, we were born lost and remain lost even if we don't realize it. Jesus came to rescue us from the futility of a life that seems well-lived in the here and now but ignores eternity. He came to purchase sinners—that's you and me—so we could be adopted into his family forever.

How did he do that? He died. The baby, so long expected and rejoiced over when he was born, came so that he could die as the perfect sacrifice for our rebellion against him. God is not sloppy in his justice; every sin must be punished. Without a substitute, we would be rightly condemned to suffer for all eternity because of our self-centeredness and desire to do what God has forbidden. There is no hope apart from God providing a way to atone for our sin. Jesus came to the earth, taking on a body, so he could be our substitute, taking the punishment our sins deserved. God rescued us from … God!

That is why the angels rejoiced. Perhaps they were the only ones who fully understood why he came; he came to seek and save *us*.

Imagine that you are swimming in the ocean, enjoying a beach vacation, and suddenly a boat comes near. A passenger throws out a lifeline and shouts to you to grab the rope. You might think, "No, I'm enjoying my time in the water. I don't need to be rescued, thank you. I can swim to shore on my own." What you don't realize is that a dangerous riptide is pulling you farther and farther from shore, so you'll never make it. Help is being offered—salvation—but you fail to understand how much you need it.

Extending the analogy, grabbing the rope means ceasing to try to make it on your own. You must trust the ability of the people on the boat to pull you in and that their intentions are good. In the same way, we must trust in the completed rescue mission of our Lord Jesus Christ; we must depend entirely on him for our rescue from sin. It may be only after your rescue that you understand how great the danger had been. If you took hold of the rope and got in the boat, you would probably be yelling to other swimmers to do the same thing. That is a description of the Christian life. We follow in our Master's footsteps—seeking the lost, explaining the way of salvation, and urging them to trust the completed work of the Lord Jesus, knowing that only he can cause someone to hear and heed the call to be saved.

I pray that this book has been helpful and encouraging, allowing you to see Christmas through the eyes of those who were there, but it would be a tragic loss if you understood the reality behind the Christmas story without "grabbing the rope" and trusting Christ for your salvation. Understanding that he came to save people who didn't love or even acknowledge him makes all the centuries of prophecy and preparation even more meaningful. Why would he do that? God describes himself this way in Exodus 34:6:

> The Lord, the Lord God, compassionate and gracious, slow to anger, and abounding in lovingkindness and truth.

It is his nature to express his love in the salvation of sinners, providing a rescue from the certainty of judgment. It is indeed good news of great joy for all people!

Acknowledgments

I thank Christ Jesus our Lord, who has strengthened
me, because He considered me faithful, putting me into
service. (1 Timothy 1:12)

I am grateful to the congregation of Bethel Baptist Church
in St. Charles, Illinois; this book flowed from sermons that I
preached there. I am blessed to be your pastor! Nicole Campo-
rese of Just My Type Transcription patiently transcribed my sermons; thank you for really listening to every word! My editors,
Liz Smith of InkSmith Editorial Services and Robyn Mulder,
took my best and made it better.

To my gracious wife, Jan: thank you for your patience and
encouragement during the process of preparing the sermons
and the book. May the Lord bless you!

About the Author

Jay was born and raised in Kansas City. Although his family attended church every week and he participated in youth group and choirs, he had never understood the gospel during those years. In the Lord's sovereignty, he joined a fraternity at the University of Kansas where he met two fraternity brothers who shared the reality of sin and forgiveness in Christ. After his first semester, Jay trusted Jesus as his Savior and Lord and became the spiritual brother of the men who witnessed to him. He joined a local church that focused on the college campus, began studying the Scriptures and teaching Bible studies—and met his future wife, Jan. They have been married for over thirty-three years, have four adult children, and are now empty nesters learning how to be good grandparents.

Jay completed a master's degree in business administration at the University of Kansas, became a certified public accountant, then joined an accounting firm in the consulting division. While pursuing a career in software development and database design, Jay continued to teach Bible studies and Sunday school classes. He most recently worked for the Blue Cross Blue Shield Association for fourteen years before moving into ministry full time. He has served as a church elder and pulpit supply speaker at several local churches. He began serving Bethel Baptist Church as pastor in June 2018. Jay enjoys learning and is pursuing a Master of Divinity degree at The Southern Baptist Theological Seminary in Louisville, Kentucky. You can listen to Jay's sermons at Bethel Baptist Church here: https://bbcstc.org.

Jay would appreciate your feedback on this book; please consider leaving an online review.

www.ingramcontent.com/pod-product-compliance
Lightning Source LLC
Chambersburg PA
CBHW030110070426
42448CB00036B/630